G000278452

No FOREIGN LAnDs

100 Of The Most Inspiring Travel Quotes Of All Time

EDITED BY DAVID S. MILLER

a book from  matador network

a book from
❧ matadornetwork™

Published in the United States by
Matador Network
P.O. Box 85
Stinson Beach, CA 94970
MatadorNetwork.com

Compilation © 2011 by Matador Network
Introduction © 2011 by David S. Miller
Cover Photo © Paul Ferraris
All rights are reserved. No part of this publication may be reproduced,
stored in a retrieval system or transmitted in any form or by any means,
electronic, mechanical, photocopying, recording or otherwise, without
prior permission of the publisher.

Matador Network is a registered trademark of Matador Ventures, LLC.

ISBN-13: 978-0615552422
ISBN-10: 0615552420

Concept: Ross Borden
Design: Bumpercrop Studio
Editorial Associates: Hal Amen, Julie Schwietert

"There is no moment of delight in any pilgrimage like the beginning of it."

– CHARLES DUDLEY WARNER

WE WERE AT THE EDGE of the pastureland where the willows were so thick you couldn't see people approaching. A man — a *gaucho* or "paisano" as he'd be called here — appeared quietly out of the grass. He emerged the way horses do, with very little noise, but just suddenly *there*. My wife was walking beside me. In the grass a few steps in front of us was our two-year-old daughter. She wasn't aware of the man. But from the way my wife remained silent, and suddenly grew tense, I could tell she'd noticed him.

For a few seconds we were all walking in the same direction and at the same pace. It didn't seem threatening exactly, and yet it was unsettling. I'd never seen him before. We'd only been down here a few months and this was a new way for us to get to town. We didn't know whose land it was. It seemed like no man's land, as is so often the case here in Patagonia.

"*Como anda señor?*" he asked.

We made eye contact then. He could've been 28 or 48. He had Mapuche Indian features and a super weathered face. He wore a beret and smiled in a way that seemed drunk or perhaps just happy at that moment. After three straight months of rain, summer was finally drying out the valley. It was mid-afternoon and a warm wind was blowing, moving around the stalks and flower heads of the lupines and thistle all around us. I smiled and nodded back, saying everything was good, relieved for some reason, and at the same time feeling a certain shame about my initial suspicion and fear.

We kept walking for another 30 seconds without saying anything. Our footsteps made soft sounds in the grass. There were huge peaks — the Andean Cordillera and the steep ridge of Piltriquitrón — on every part of the horizon. For a second it felt as if we were in a giant amphitheater, and our movement across the valley floor was strangely stage-like, all of us stepping in the same rhythm set by my daughter out in front. The man said something which I couldn't understand except the phrase "*la chiquita.*" But he said it in a way that seemed from one father to another. He was looking at Layla and still smiling.

Then he turned and disappeared into the grass.

....

As with all of my travels, our time here in Patagonia would be difficult to characterize, or reduce to a single "takeaway." What I'll remember are *moments*. This is the way travel reveals itself. Each moment on the arc of a journey connects to and builds on other moments. The meaning may not be fully understood until long after we've come home. Or it may not be understood at all. Oftentimes it's as if experiencing the moment in and of itself was the point.

No Foreign Lands is a book about moments. Each of the 100 quotes collected here takes only a moment to read, and perhaps only took the author a moment to write or to say, but points towards a lifetime of experience.

Our title is borrowed from a passage in one of Robert Louis Stevenson's memoirs: "There is no foreign land; it is the traveller only that is foreign." This is an underlying theme both for the book and for our editorial vision overall. While much travel writing historically and today focuses on the "exotic" nature of other people, places, and cultures, *No Foreign Lands* explores how people are simply people, place is simply place, everywhere you go. For a traveler to regard people and places as "foreign" is to objectify them. These quotes remind us to see the world, as travel writer Mark Jenkins says, "the way it is, not the way you imagine it."

There is a second layer to the title, however. Over the last decade, the internet has given us the ability to travel almost anywhere, to connect with other travelers as well as locals, and to transform our journeys into media with the power to reach millions. This has made way for an unprecedented "travel culture" worldwide. We have entered an age where not only being "world travelers," but feeling very much at home in the cultures and native languages of multiple countries, has become the everyday reality of thousands of people. Collectively, we form a nation of permanent travelers. This is no better exemplified than by the photographers whose work features in this book, several of whom are raising multilingual, multicultural families, working, living, and traveling far from where they were born. Among many of us is a growing sense that there really are no "foreign lands" out there, but simply more places, people, and cultures to get to know.

The quotes in *No Foreign Lands* are organized into five sections. These are not intended as rigid categories but rather to suggest general themes and associations between different elements of travel.

MOMENT is about thresholds, about defining moments in our journeys, and how travel relates to perception, memory, and identity.

PEOPLE recognizes the different ways we see others, and the relationships we create while traveling. It's about lessons learned from other cultures, and how they're carried home, giving new perspectives on where we're from.

TERRAIN looks at the topography of a journey, and how it's inspired and ultimately informed by our connection to the land and the ways we explore it.

TRANSPORT is about getting from one place to another, the pleasures and suffering, the romanticism and reality of being on the road.

PLAY reflects on the example given us by children: to make yourself at home wherever you go. It's a reminder how lightheartedness, folly, and foolishness will always be at the center of travel.

The idea isn't to present a single book of travel "adages" but a diverse collection. Some of the quotes look at travel philosophically and have a feel of great distance from the journeys they describe, a kind of "summing up" of travel. Others are immediate, uttered spontaneously, and refer to specific places and moments. And still others are taken from novels, poems, songs, and speeches which develop new layers of meaning and inspiration in the context of travel.

The quotes are juxtaposed with photos taken everywhere from Cuba to the Himalaya to San Francisco Bay. As with the general organization of the categories, the pictures are less about "illustrating" the quotes as they are about creating an interplay, a suggested narrative, a space for the reader's imagination to enter. Photographers' notes about each shot are found at the end of the book, as well as a bibliography. Above all, *No Foreign Lands* is meant to travel, to accompany you on the road. We wanted to keep it small and packable, available in the moment.

....

I ended up only seeing the gaucho once more out there in the pastureland. It was just another quick nod as I was walking to town, nothing exceptional about it other than the fact that we recognized each other now. Since then the willows that flanked the fields have been cut down and it's all open. In two years this place has changed so much. One day the memories of these moments will be all that remains.

— David S. Miller
10/19/2011
Patagonia, Argentina

"Real adventure is defined best as a journey from which you may not come back alive, and certainly not as the same person."
– YVON CHOUINARD

"A good traveler has no fixed plans and is not intent on arriving."

– LAO TZU

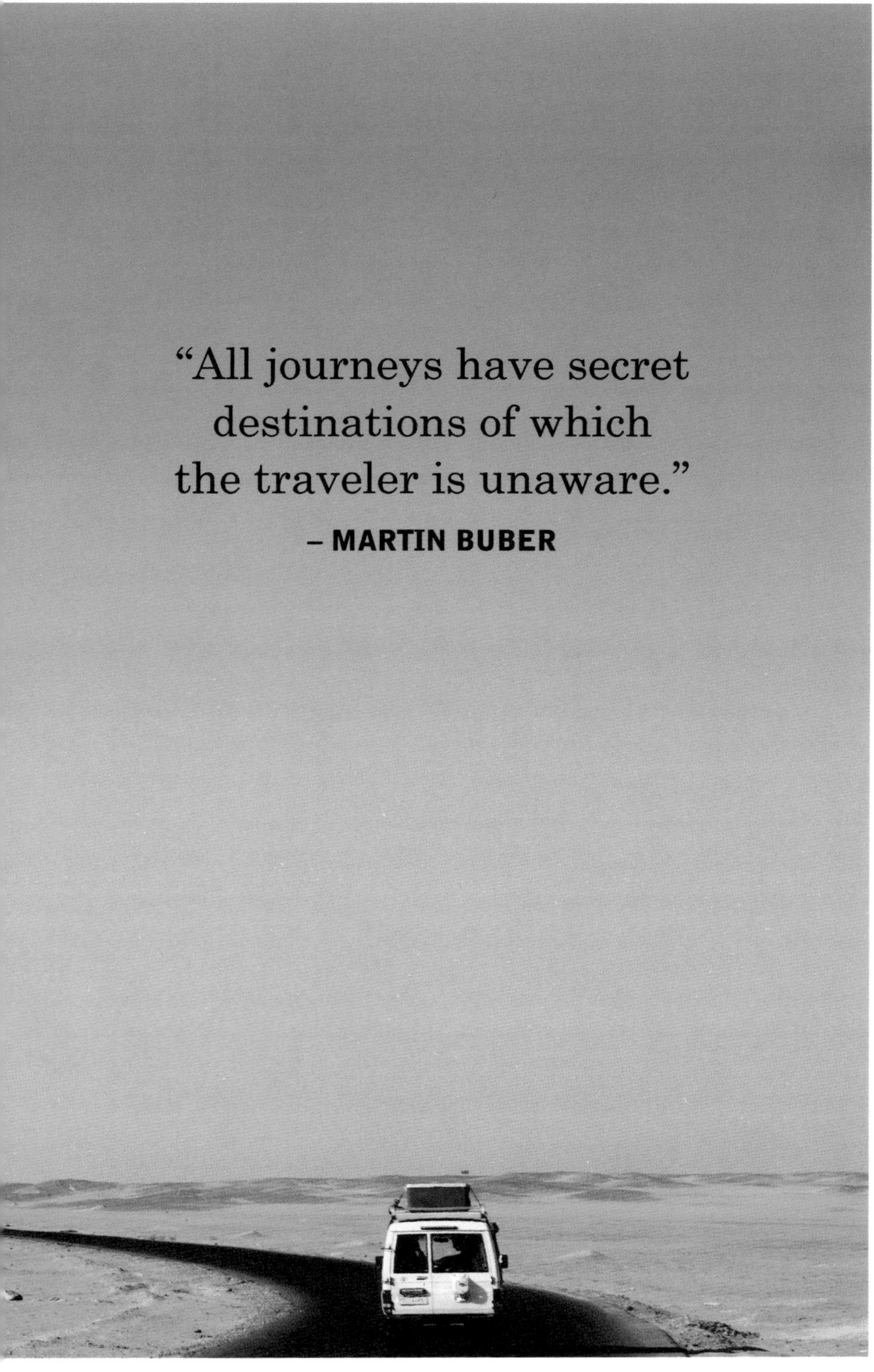

"All journeys have secret
destinations of which
the traveler is unaware."

– MARTIN BUBER

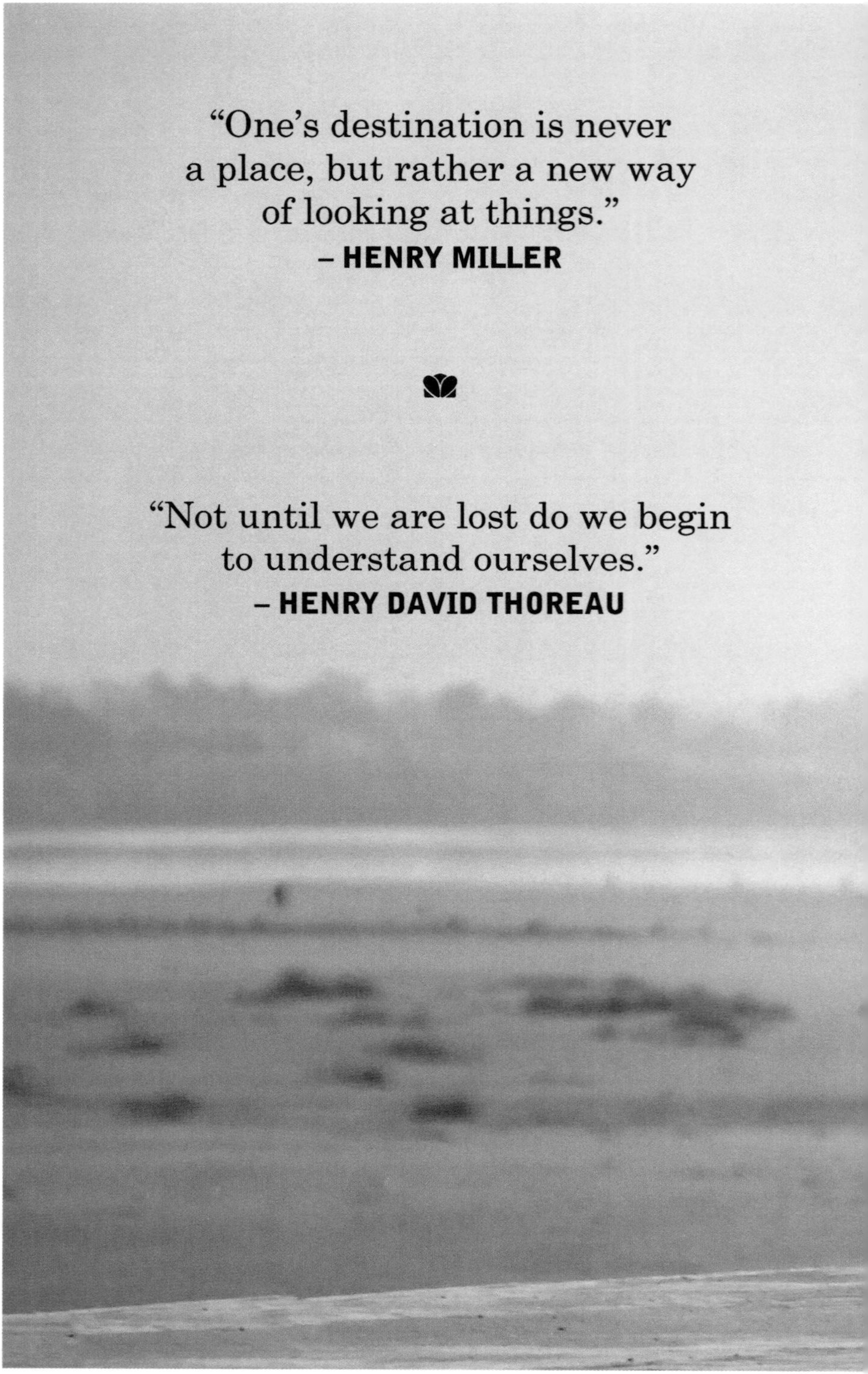

"One's destination is never
a place, but rather a new way
of looking at things."
– HENRY MILLER

🐾

"Not until we are lost do we begin
to understand ourselves."
– HENRY DAVID THOREAU

"The real voyage of discovery consists not in seeking new landscapes, but in having new eyes."
– MARCEL PROUST

"The birds have vanished down the sky.
Now the last cloud drains away.
We sit together, the mountain and me,
until only the mountain remains."
– **"Zazen on Ching-t'ing Mountain" by LI PO
(translated by Sam Hamill)**

"He was alone.
He was unheeded,
happy and near to
the wild heart of life."
– JAMES JOYCE, A Portrait
of the Artist as a Young Man

"Like all great travelers,
I have seen more than I remember,
and remember more than I have seen."
– BENJAMIN DISRAELI

"A journey is like marriage. The certain way to be wrong is to think you control it."
– **JOHN STEINBECK**

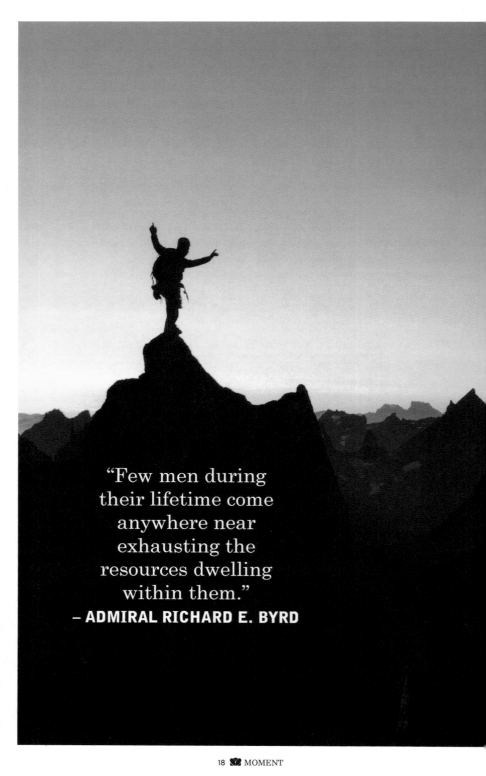

"Few men during their lifetime come anywhere near exhausting the resources dwelling within them."
– ADMIRAL RICHARD E. BYRD

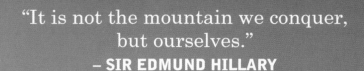

"It is not the mountain we conquer,
but ourselves."
– SIR EDMUND HILLARY

"We only become what we are by
the radical and deep-seated refusal
of that which others have made of us."
– JEAN-PAUL SARTRE

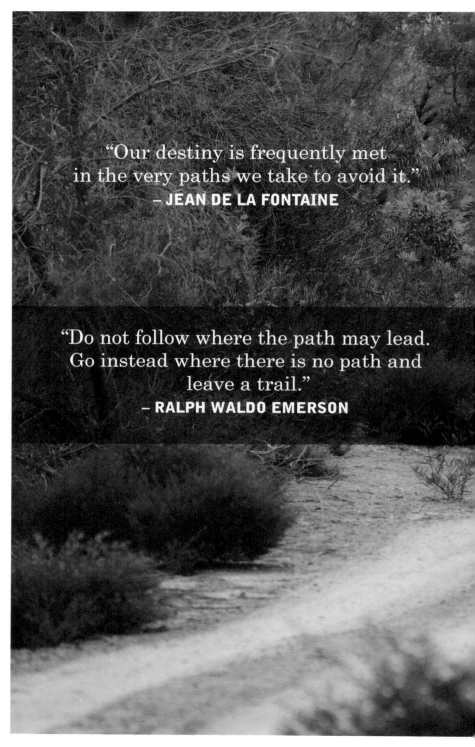

"Our destiny is frequently met in the very paths we take to avoid it."
– JEAN DE LA FONTAINE

"Do not follow where the path may lead. Go instead where there is no path and leave a trail."
– RALPH WALDO EMERSON

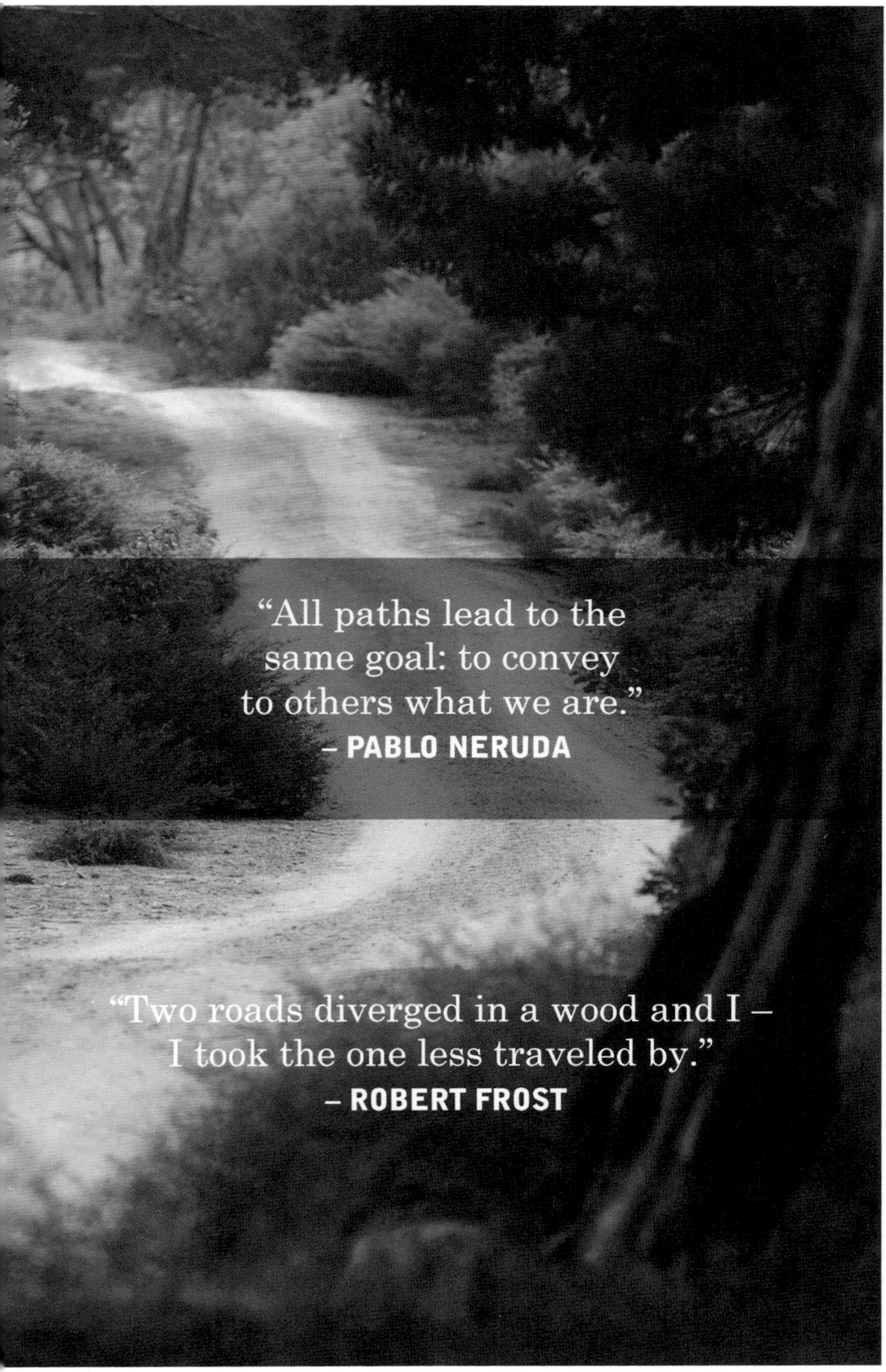
"All paths lead to the same goal: to convey to others what we are."
– PABLO NERUDA
"Two roads diverged in a wood and I – I took the one less traveled by."
– ROBERT FROST

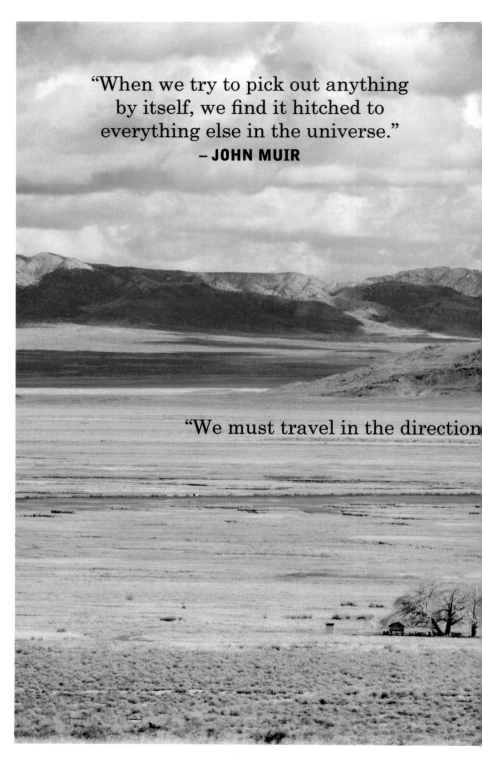

"When we try to pick out anything by itself, we find it hitched to everything else in the universe."
– JOHN MUIR

"We must travel in the direction

"Sick on my journey,
only my dreams will wander
these desolate moors."
— **Death Poem of MATSUO BASHŌ**

of our fear."   **— JOHN BERRYMAN**

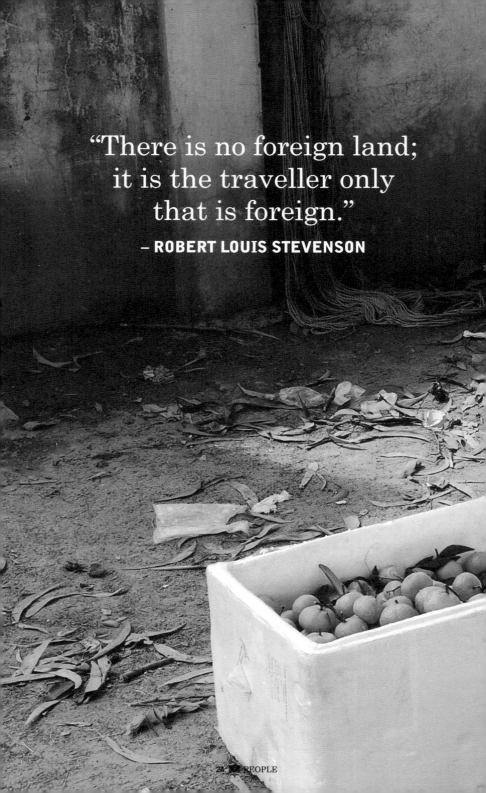

"There is no foreign land;
it is the traveller only
that is foreign."

– ROBERT LOUIS STEVENSON

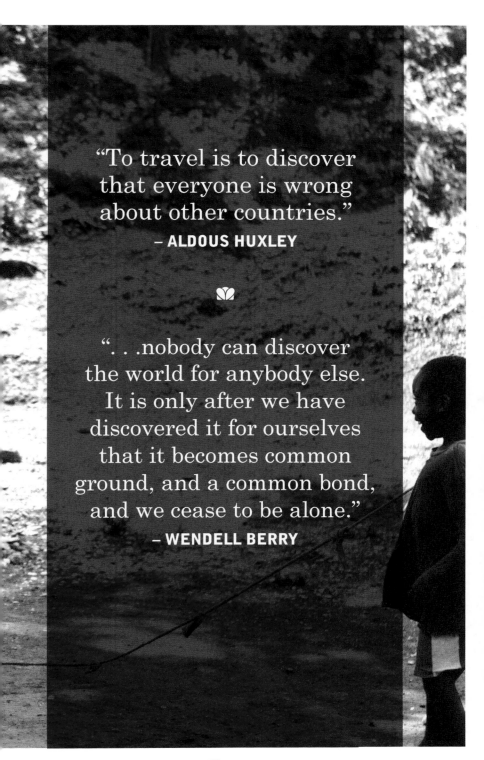

"To travel is to discover
that everyone is wrong
about other countries."
– ALDOUS HUXLEY

". . .nobody can discover
the world for anybody else.
It is only after we have
discovered it for ourselves
that it becomes common
ground, and a common bond,
and we cease to be alone."
– WENDELL BERRY

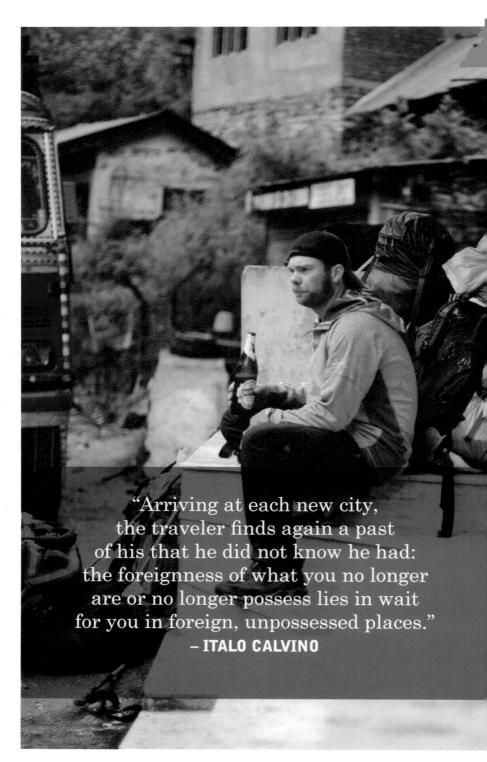

"Arriving at each new city,
the traveler finds again a past
of his that he did not know he had:
the foreignness of what you no longer
are or no longer possess lies in wait
for you in foreign, unpossessed places."
— **ITALO CALVINO**

"One always begins to forgive a place
as soon as it's left behind."
– **CHARLES DICKENS**

"Who says that the dead do not think of us?
Wherever I go she travels with me."
– **MEI YAO CH'EN (translated by Kenneth Rexroth)**

"Travel is fatal to prejudice, bigotry, and narrow-mindedness."
– **MARK TWAIN**

"Perhaps travel cannot prevent bigotry, but by demonstrating that all peoples cry, laugh, eat, worry, and die, it can introduce the idea that if we try and understand each other, we may even become friends."

– MAYA ANGELOU

"Don't tell me how educated you are, tell me how much you traveled."
— **MOHAMMED**

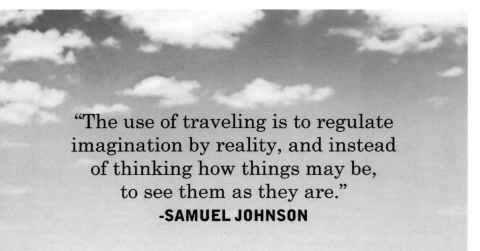

"The use of traveling is to regulate imagination by reality, and instead of thinking how things may be, to see them as they are."
-SAMUEL JOHNSON

"A journey is best measured in friends, rather than miles."
– TIM CAHILL

"If you reject the food, ignore the customs, fear the religion and avoid the people, you might better stay at home."
– JAMES MICHENER

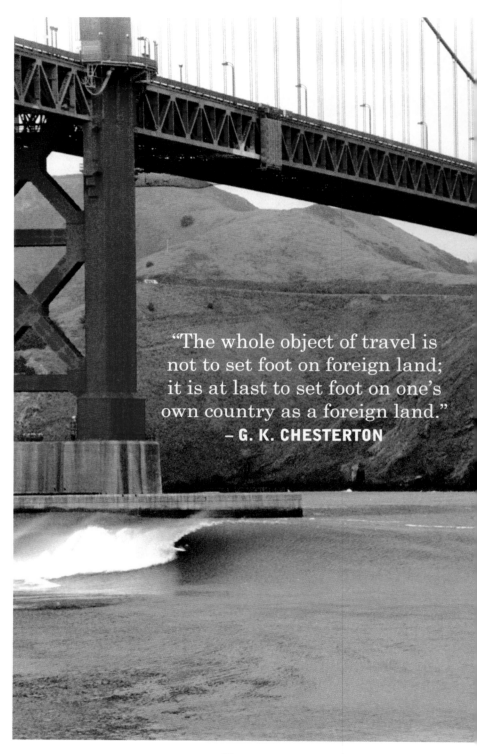

"The whole object of travel is not to set foot on foreign land; it is at last to set foot on one's own country as a foreign land."
— **G. K. CHESTERTON**

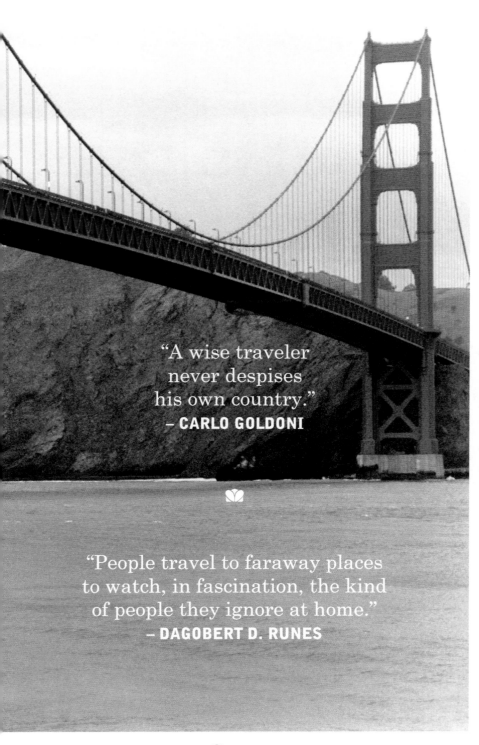

"A wise traveler
never despises
his own country."
– CARLO GOLDONI

"People travel to faraway places
to watch, in fascination, the kind
of people they ignore at home."
– DAGOBERT D. RUNES

"For so many centuries, the exchange of gifts has held us together. It has made it possible to bridge the abyss where language struggles."
– **BARRY LOPEZ**

"As the traveler who has once been from home is wiser than he who has never left his own doorstep, so a knowledge of one other culture should sharpen our ability to scrutinize more steadily, to appreciate more lovingly, our own."
— **MARGARET MEAD**

". . .love having no geography,
knows no boundaries."
– **TRUMAN CAPOTE**

"When you're traveling, you
are what you are. People don't
have your past to hold against you.
No yesterdays on the road."
– **WILLIAM LEAST HEAT MOON**

"Even in Siberia there is happiness."
– From "In Exile" by **ANTON CHEKHOV**

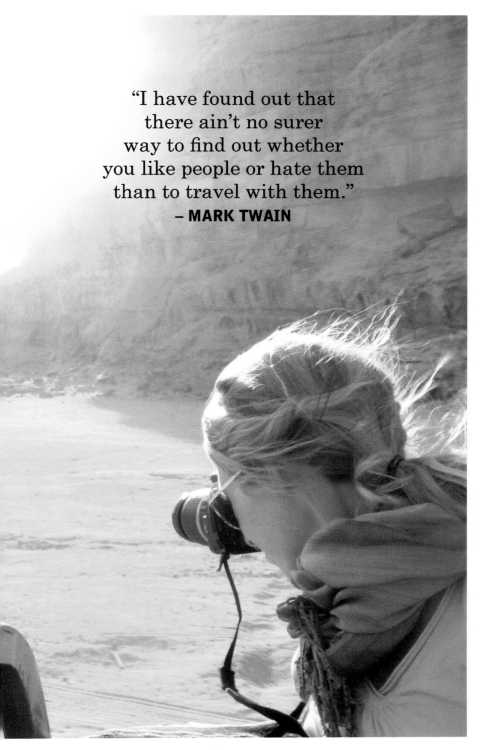

"I have found out that there ain't no surer way to find out whether you like people or hate them than to travel with them."
– **MARK TWAIN**

"The soul is no traveller;
the wise man stays at home,
and when his necessities,
his duties, on any occasion call
him from his house or into
foreign lands, he is at home still . . ."
– RALPH WALDO EMERSON

"I have walked through many lives, some of

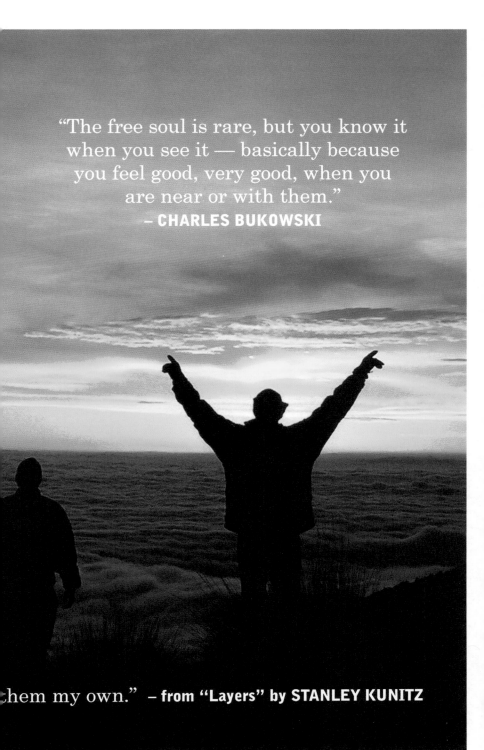

"The free soul is rare, but you know it when you see it — basically because you feel good, very good, when you are near or with them."
– CHARLES BUKOWSKI

:hem my own." **– from "Layers" by STANLEY KUNITZ**

"The earth and myself
are of one mind."

– CHIEF JOSEPH

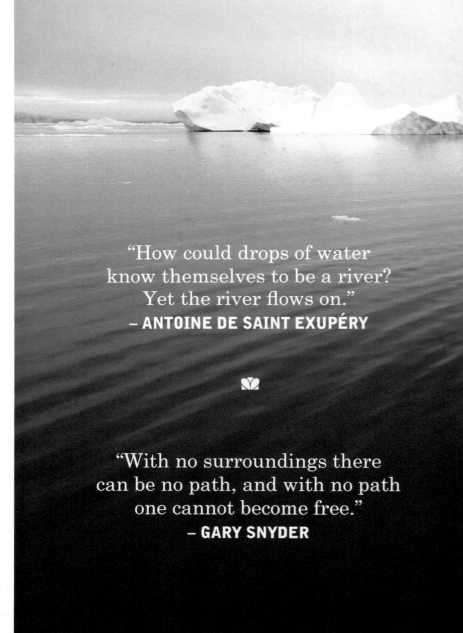

"How could drops of water
know themselves to be a river?
Yet the river flows on."
– ANTOINE DE SAINT EXUPÉRY

"With no surroundings there
can be no path, and with no path
one cannot become free."
– GARY SNYDER

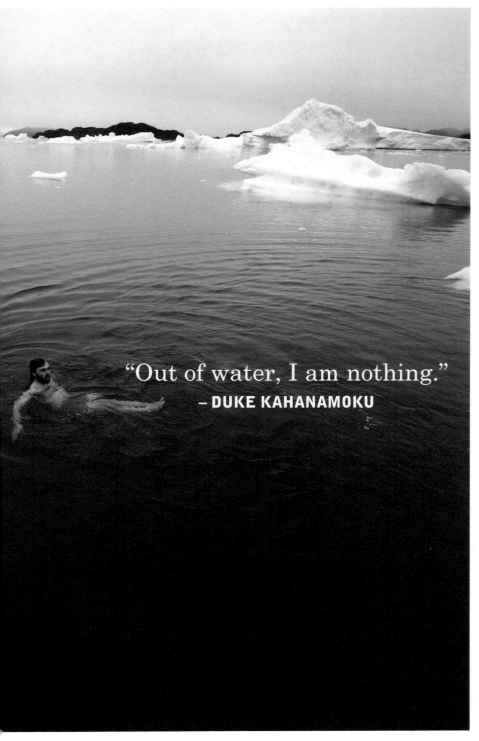

"Out of water, I am nothing."
– **DUKE KAHANAMOKU**

"It is not down in any map;
true places never are."
— **HERMAN MELVILLE**

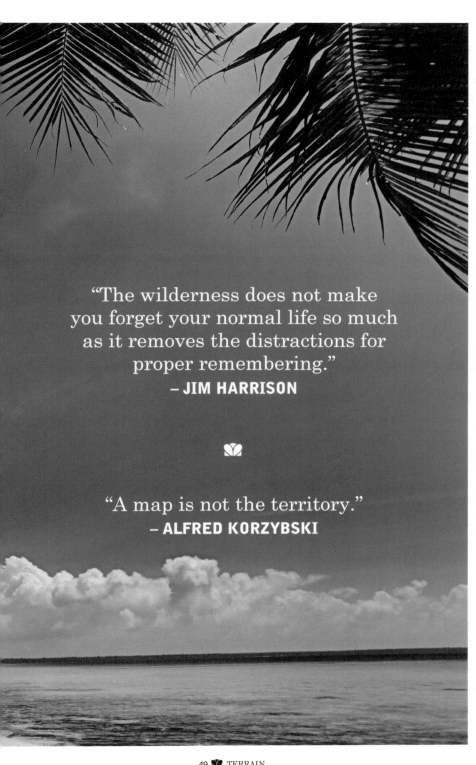

"The wilderness does not make you forget your normal life so much as it removes the distractions for proper remembering."
– **JIM HARRISON**

"A map is not the territory."
– **ALFRED KORZYBSKI**

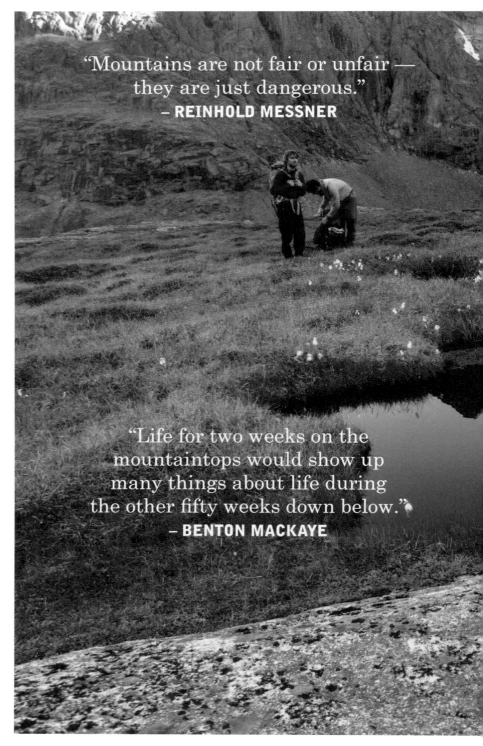

"Mountains are not fair or unfair —
they are just dangerous."
– **REINHOLD MESSNER**

"Life for two weeks on the
mountaintops would show up
many things about life during
the other fifty weeks down below."
– **BENTON MACKAYE**

"Because it's there."
— **GEORGE MALLORY**
**(member of first British expeditions
to climb Mt. Everest), on why he
wanted to climb the mountain**

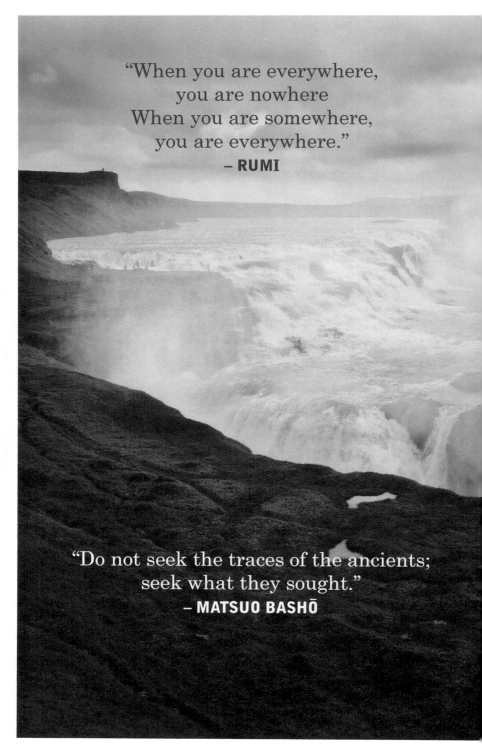

"When you are everywhere,
you are nowhere
When you are somewhere,
you are everywhere."
– RUMI

"Do not seek the traces of the ancients;
seek what they sought."
– MATSUO BASHŌ

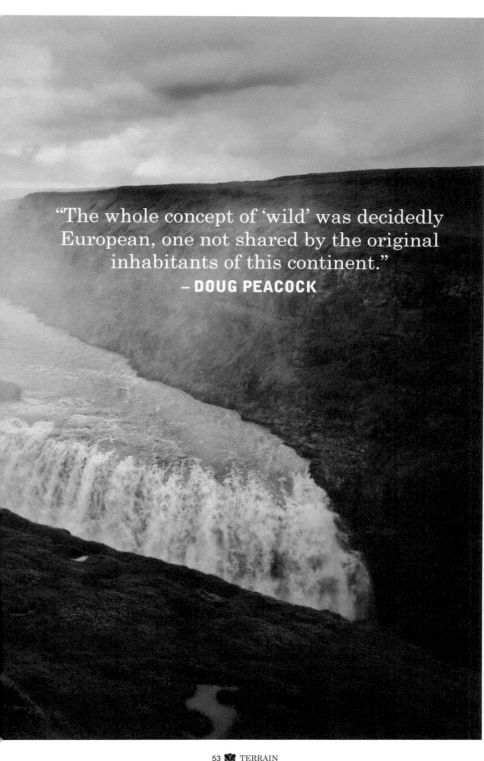

"The whole concept of 'wild' was decidedly European, one not shared by the original inhabitants of this continent."
– **DOUG PEACOCK**

"We come and go,
but the land is always here."
— **WILLA CATHER**

"...before the traveler sees the ocean,
he feels a stirring in his blood."
— **JORGE LUIS BORGES**

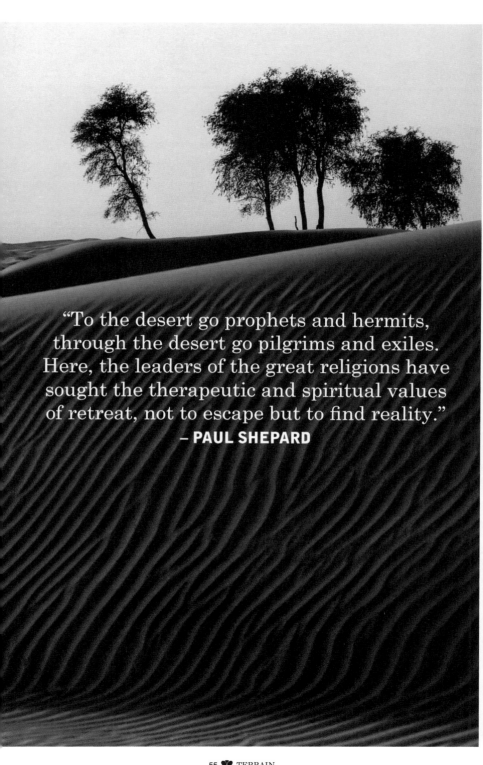

"To the desert go prophets and hermits, through the desert go pilgrims and exiles. Here, the leaders of the great religions have sought the therapeutic and spiritual values of retreat, not to escape but to find reality."
– PAUL SHEPARD

"The soil you see is not ordinary soil —
it is the dust of the blood, flesh, and
bones of our ancestors."
– "CURLY," Crow Scout of General Custer

"The world the way it is,
not the way you imagine it."
– MARK JENKINS

"The civilized man
has built a coach, but
has lost use of his feet."

– RALPH WALDO EMERSON

"Our battered suitcases were piled on the sidewalk again; we had longer ways to go. But no matter, the road is life."
– From On the Road, JACK KEROUAC

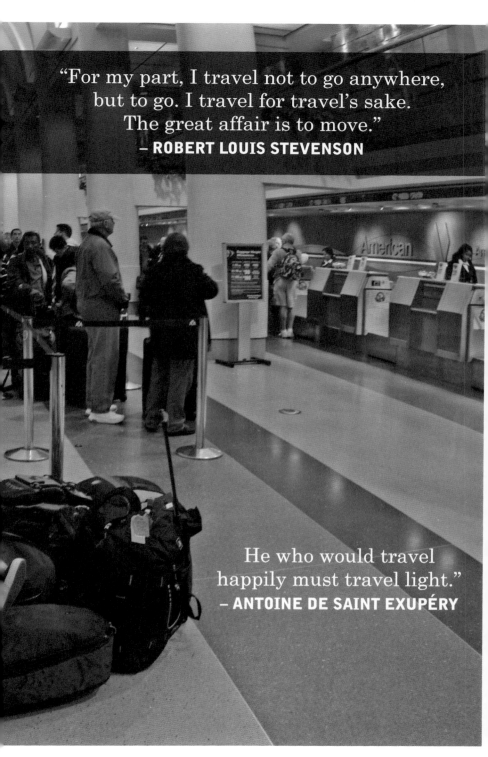

"For my part, I travel not to go anywhere, but to go. I travel for travel's sake. The great affair is to move."
– ROBERT LOUIS STEVENSON

He who would travel happily must travel light."
– ANTOINE DE SAINT EXUPÉRY

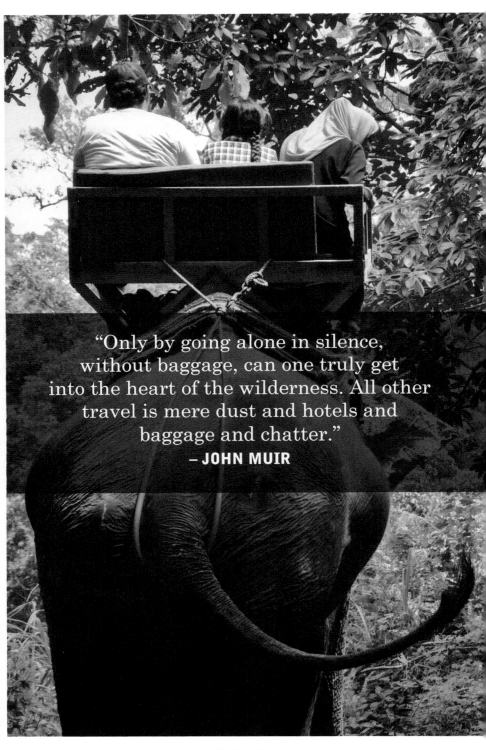

"Only by going alone in silence, without baggage, can one truly get into the heart of the wilderness. All other travel is mere dust and hotels and baggage and chatter."

– JOHN MUIR

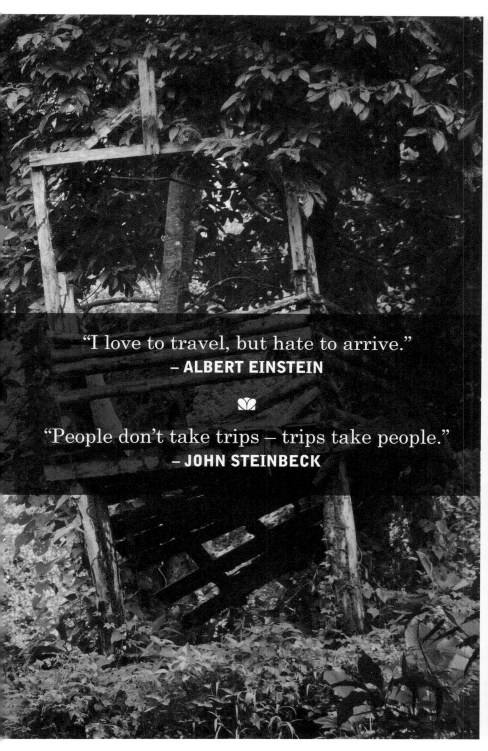

"I love to travel, but hate to arrive."
– ALBERT EINSTEIN

"People don't take trips – trips take people."
– JOHN STEINBECK

"To awaken quite alone in a strange town is one of the pleasantest sensations in the world."
– FREYA STARK

"It's a battered old suitcase and a hotel someplace and a wound that will never heal."
– TOM WAITS

"He who has seen one cathedral ten times has seen something; he who has seen ten cathedrals once has seen but little; and he who has spent half an hour in each of a hundred cathedrals has seen nothing at all."
– SINCLAIR LEWIS,
on sightseeing

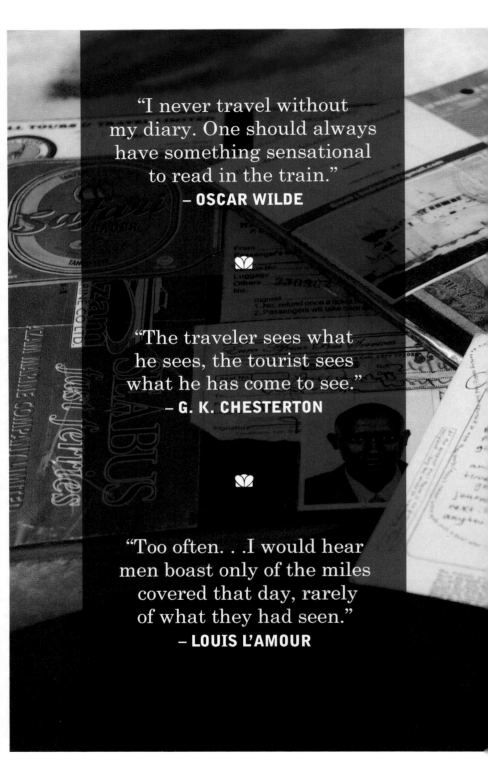

"I never travel without my diary. One should always have something sensational to read in the train."
– **OSCAR WILDE**

"The traveler sees what he sees, the tourist sees what he has come to see."
– **G. K. CHESTERTON**

"Too often. . .I would hear men boast only of the miles covered that day, rarely of what they had seen."
– **LOUIS L'AMOUR**

"When you travel, remember that
a foreign country is not designed to
make you comfortable. It is designed
to make its own people comfortable."
– CLIFTON FADIMAN

"Is anything sadder than a train
That leaves when it's supposed to,
That has only one voice,
Only one route?"
– PRIMO LEVI, from "Monday"

"One main factor in the upward trend of animal life has been the power of wandering."
– **ALFRED NORTH WHITEHEAD**

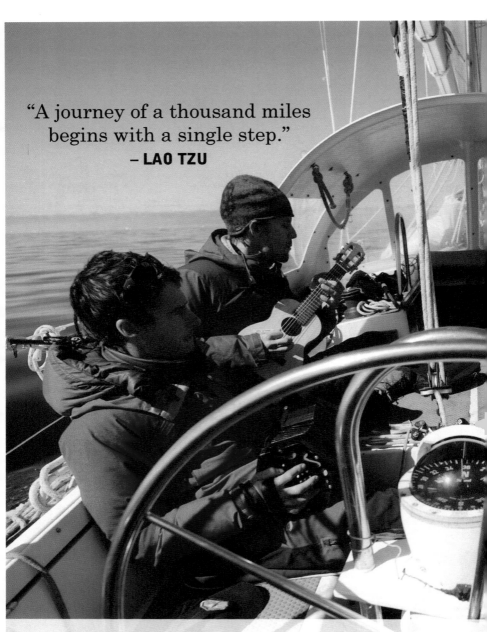

"A journey of a thousand miles begins with a single step."
— LAO TZU

"A child on a farm sees a plane fly overhead and dreams of a faraway place. A traveler on the

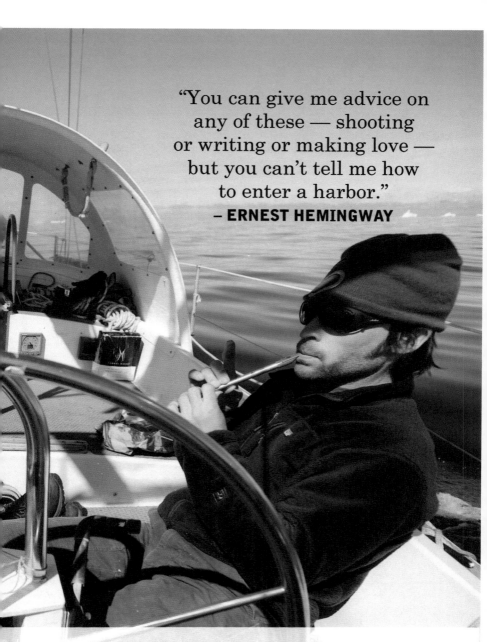

"You can give me advice on any of these — shooting or writing or making love — but you can't tell me how to enter a harbor."
— **ERNEST HEMINGWAY**

plane sees the farmhouse...and thinks of home."
— **CARL BURNS**

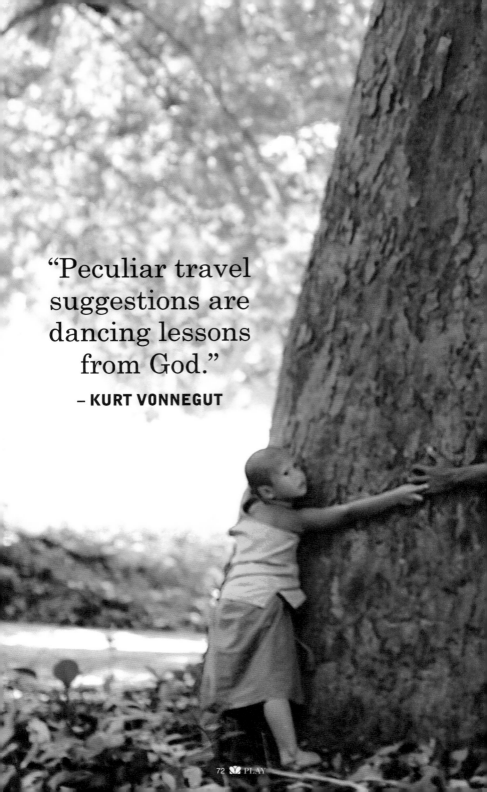

"Peculiar travel suggestions are dancing lessons from God."

— **KURT VONNEGUT**

"Afoot and light-hearted I take to the open road,
Healthy, free, the world before me,
The long brown path before me
leading wherever I choose."
– WALT WHITMAN

"Every perfect traveler
always creates the country
where he travels."
–NIKOS KAZANTZAKIS

"It is by riding a bicycle that you
learn the contours of a country best,
since you have to sweat up the hills
and can coast down them."
– ERNEST HEMINGWAY

"Twenty years from now you
will be more disappointed by the
things you didn't do than by the ones
you did do. So throw off the bowlines,
sail away from the safe harbor.
Catch the trade winds in your sails.
Explore. Dream. Discover."
– MARK TWAIN

"Half the fun of the travel
is the aesthetic of lostness."
– RAY BRADBURY

"I haven't been everywhere,
but it's on my list."
– SUSAN SONTAG

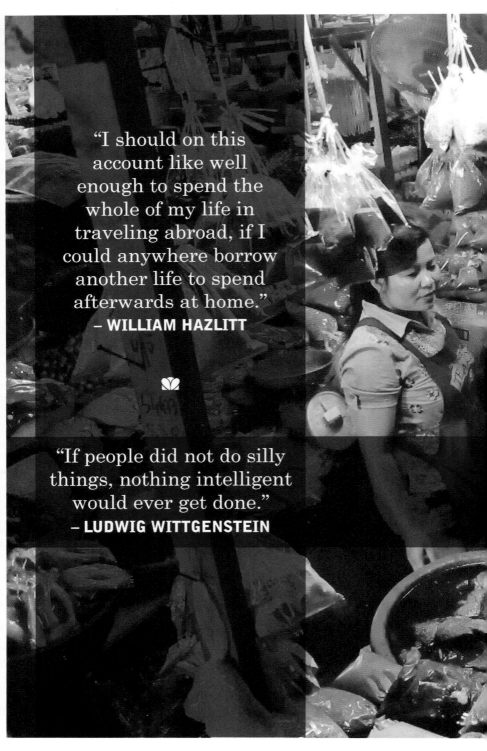

"I should on this account like well enough to spend the whole of my life in traveling abroad, if I could anywhere borrow another life to spend afterwards at home."
– WILLIAM HAZLITT

"If people did not do silly things, nothing intelligent would ever get done."
– LUDWIG WITTGENSTEIN

"The first condition of understanding a foreign country is to smell it."
— T. S. ELIOT

"You can discover more about
a person in an hour of play than
in a year of conversation."
– PLATO

"No valid plans for the future
can be made by those who have
no capacity for living now."
– ALAN WATTS

"To my mind, the greatest reward and luxury of travel is to be able to experience everyday things as if for the first time, to be in a position in which almost nothing is so familiar it is taken for granted."
— **BILL BRYSON**

"I should not care to revisit all these fair places of the world except in the fashion I visited them before. GLASS IN HAND!"
– JACK LONDON

"I may not have gone where I intended to go, but I think I have ended up where I needed to be."
— **DOUGLAS ADAMS**

"We start going downhill,
when we stop taking risks."
– LAIRD HAMILTON

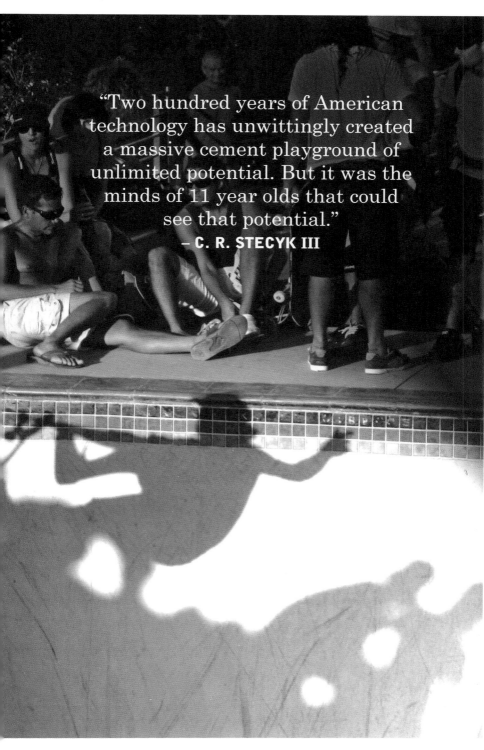

"Two hundred years of American technology has unwittingly created a massive cement playground of unlimited potential. But it was the minds of 11 year olds that could see that potential."
— C. R. STECYK III

"If everything seems
under control, you're just
not going fast enough."
– MARIO ANDRETTI

"On my tombstone they will carve,

"IT NEVER GOT FAST ENOUGH FOR ME."
— HUNTER S. THOMPSON

FRONT COVER:
"Early morning boat ride on the Ganges River, Varanasi, India. After snapping this photo I was stunned by a pod of freshwater dolphins."
– Paul Ferraris

(PAGE) 3:
"Riding the streets of Phnom Penh, Cambodia, in a traditional tuk-tuk. It's a quintessential and familiar travel shot, but there's still an element of excitement that seeing a different country from this angle brings."
– Lola Akinmade-Åkerström

8-9:
"Pat Goodman sits atop Peak 5394 after its first ascent via the route 'Indian Beauty Queen,' which took two days of climbing after two weeks of waiting to establish. Pat and I were joined by Freddie Wilkinson and Janet Bergman."
– Ben Ditto

10-11:
"Just outside of Hurghada, Egypt, as we rode in a convoy into the Eastern Desert, the scene in front of me — miles of sand meeting blue sky — seemed a metaphor for our journey and travel in general. We may not know where we're going, but if we go with the flow (in this case, the road), we'll get somewhere special and experience something new."
– Lola Akinmade-Åkerström

12-13:
"This candid shot was taken in Vientiane, along the Mekong River facing Thailand. This Buddhist monk was chatting with a young backpacker who seemed fascinated by his words."
– Daniel Nahabedian

14-15:
"Olivier Favresse swings off the last pitch of the 'Impossible Wall' route in Greenland's Sortehul Fjord. Favresse, along with his brother Nicolas, Sean Villanueva O'Driscoll, and myself, made the first ascent of the 20-pitch big wall in 12 days. The foursome accessed the wall directly from the deck of the 33' *Dodo's Delight*, captained by Scotsman Bob Shepton. This expedition lasted three months and established nine first ascents, winning the 2011 Piolet d'Or award. At the expedition's end we sailed back across the North Atlantic to Scotland."
– Ben Ditto

16-17:

"Olivier Favresse (red jacket) and Sean Villanueva O'Driscoll (both from Belgium) hold on for dear life aboard the 33' *Dodo's Delight*. After a three-month big walling expedition in Greenland, we crossed the North Atlantic and faced several post-tropical storms along the 1500-mile open ocean passage."
– Ben Ditto

18-19:

"Sunrise on the southern tip of Greenland."
– Ben Ditto

20-21:

"A dirt road leaves the Stapylton Campground in the Grampian Mountains of Victoria, Australia."
– Ben Ditto

22-23:

"A hot day in western Utah's Fish Spring National Wildlife Refuge. I've spent many days photographing in this area for the sake of representing the water and wildlife communities found in the arid great basin."
– Ben Ditto

24-25:

"While exploring Silk Village outside of Phnom Penh, I ran into a fruit and vegetable vendor. I loved how the colors around her contrasted with the background and raised my camera in a gesture that asked, "Can I take your photograph?" This was the result."
– Lola Akinmade-Åkerström

26-27:

"Haitian kids jump rope just outside the town of Jacmel."
– Cody Forest Doucette

28-29:

"Pat Goodman awaits a ride in Manikaran, India (Parvati Valley). Pat is likely soaking wet, for we had just bailed (along with Freddie Wilkinson and Janet Bergman) from an attempt to climb high above town on some unclimbed granite spires. There were some big cold storms that covered the faces with snow, so we had to go back to town to allow conditions to stabilize."
– Ben Ditto

30-31:
"We were in Nicaragua volunteering as photojournalists with World Hope and spent one of our days off in Catarina. While there, I spotted a couple nuns, who I then proceeded to stalk for a while until they agreed to my snapping their photo. When I was done, I showed them the shot in the viewfinder, and my friend Cheryl Black caught this moment."
— Lola Akinmade-Åkerström

32-33:
"Outside of Debre Sina in Ethiopia, I found this schoolboy reading on the ridge overlooking a sea of small sustainable farms."
— Paul Ferraris

34-35:
"I'd previously noticed these two boys trailing us as we made our way back to the boat. When our boat was getting ready to leave Silk Village (Cambodia), they clung to its wooden rails, almost reaching in. They were as curious of me as I was of them. The boy on the left with the missing teeth caught my attention. His eyes seemed to be saying 'Why are you leaving so soon? You haven't scratched the surface of my village?'"
— Lola Akinmade-Åkerström

36-37:
"Bryan is a great tube rider and one of the few soft-spoken regulars who frequent this very recognizable spot."
— Paul Ferraris

38-39:
"Himba family near Opuwo, Namibia. I always feel awkward taking pictures of people, but once the Polaroid comes out, it is always a free-for-all. These guys had a blast and we all walked away with something special."
— Paul Ferraris

40-41:
"Riding in the bed of a Bedouin's pickup over the sand of Wadi Rum, Jordan. Looking west. I always enjoy photographing my photographer wife, especially when she doesn't know I'm doing it."
— Hal Amen

42-43:
"Halfway up 6075m Vulcan Misti near Arequipa, Peru. Misti is an active volcano and a fun but not-to-be-underestimated climb. Moments after this photo was taken, the clouds swept up the mountain and we were engulfed in a violent storm with high winds

and hail that left a thick dusting of snow on the mountain above us. We would summit the next day with close to zero visibility."
– Ross Borden

44-45:
"Kitt Doucette stands in the shadow of the ancients in the Rano Raraku quarry on the island of Rapa Nui."
– Cody Forest Doucette

46-47:
"Sean Villanueva O'Driscoll swims with icebergs formed from the Greenland ice sheet, near Upernavik, West Greenland."
– Ben Ditto

48-49:
"Ant Atoll, 30 miles off the coast of Pohnpei, Micronesia, and uninhabited. When the waves at Pohnpei went flat, we boated out to the Atolls, gathered a dozen or so coconut crabs, then roasted them over dry palms and feasted."
– Paul Ferraris

50-51:
"Returning to the boat from a long push with two new routes established in Greenland."
– Ben Ditto

52-53:
"This shot was taken at Gullfoss, meaning 'Golden Falls,' in the southwest of Iceland. Part of the 'Golden Circle,' including the geysers and Thingvellir National Park, it is one of the biggest waterfalls in Iceland."
– Daniel Nahabedian

54-55:
"Camping in the United Arab Emirates desert during the 'winter.' This was taken during sunset when the light creates strong shadows, accentuating the wrinkles on the dunes. I have always found the desert to be a mystical, serene, and relaxing place. Silence reigns, enabling us to hear those important voices inside ourselves."
– Daniel Nahabedian

56-57:
"A profile of my husband Hal Amen, on a hike up to the Chacaltaya Glacier just outside La Paz, Bolivia. The peak in the background is Wayna Potosí (6,088m / 19,974ft)."
– Aya Padrón

58-59:

"Kuchi children try to push-start a minivan in Kabul in late October 2010. Violent clashes between Kuchi herders and Hazarra farmers in Kabul prompted the local government to place hundreds of Kuchi men, women and children at Darulaman Palace for the winter. Gathering supplies to stay warm in the abandoned, dilapidated structure calls for resourcefulness. Procuring the minivan was a feat in itself for a ragged bunch of 14-year-old Afghan nomads — now if they could only get it started."
– Daniel C. Britt

60-61:

"Rusty Long naps in LAX after our flight is delayed."
– Cody Forest Doucette

62-63:

"In Mae Taeng, near Chiang Mai. I was invited to the Elephant Park to take photos and help raise money to build a hospital for rescued elephants."
– Daniel Nahabedian

64-65:

"It's easy to get lost among the ornate tombs of the Cementerio de la Recoleta in Buenos Aires, even on a sunny day when you're one among dozens or hundreds of other tourists-with-camera."
– Aya Padrón

66-67:

"Traveling from Cape Town to Cairo on public transport and occasional prayer, I would keep journals of my experiences every night. By the time I left Sudan for Egypt, I had filled four books and collected dozens of scraps of paper."
– Richard Stupart

68-69:

"I tagged along on a 3-hour dog-sled ride that took us across frozen Lake Skabram in Swedish Lapland. Surrounded by layers of snow and pine trees eerily coated in white, the reddish-orange of our supply bag popped against the icy background, providing a warm yet sharp contrast."
– Lola Akinmade-Åkerström

70-71:

"Aboard the *Dodo's Delight*, Sean Villanueva O'Driscoll and Olivier and Nicolas Favresse (left, Nico plays the small guitar) jam in the Baffin Strait."
– Ben Ditto

72-73:

"Three monks hugging a tree in a special forest temple called Wat Suan Mokkh. The temple was founded by Buddha Dasa ('slave of the Buddha'), who is like the Martin Luther of Thailand, having translated sacred Pali Buddhists texts into Thai so common people could read them for themselves."
– Ryan Libre

74-75:

"A young woman selling fruit along the Avenue du Baobab near Morondava, Western Madagascar. Chameleons are found throughout the dry grass and trees here."
– Ross Borden

76-77:

"Heading back to the *Dodo's Delight* after a few days in base camp along Greenland's west coast, near Upernavik.
– Ben Ditto

78-79:

"The market in Luang Prabang, Laos, has acres of nothing but spices and chile powders. It is definitely one of the craziest markets I've ever seen."
– Cody Forest Doucette

80-81:

"Laos seems a bit like heaven: the laughter is often and sincere; the rivers are cool and clean; and the food is healthy and local."
– Ryan Libre

82-83:

"Pavones, Costa Rica, is one of the longest Lefts in the world."
– Paul Ferraris

84-85:

"A skater airs out the bowl for the camera in Bondi Beach, Sydney, Australia."
– Cody Forest Doucette

86-87:

"Traversing the Australian Outback sometime in 2004. There was something about the blue, cloudless sky and the loneliness of the scene that seemed to sum up my experiences there."
– Paul Sullivan

FINAL SHOT:

"Honolulu International. Medium-format, tripod-mounted photo taken on an overnight layover."
– Paul Ferraris

PHOTOGRAPHERS

Lola Akinmade Åkerström is an award-winning writer and photographer who has dispatched from six continents for many major publications around the world. She is also an artist, cartoonist, and programmer, and is based in Stockholm, Sweden. **akinmade.com**

Hal Amen travels and writes and photographs. Mostly though, he spends long periods of time at the computer, editing Matador Trips.

Ross Borden is the co-founder and CEO of Matador Network. He has lived in Spain, Kenya and Argentina and currently splits time between New York and his native San Francisco.

Daniel C. Britt spent most of 2009 living on the ground in Iraq during the U.S. withdrawal from cities. In 2010 his travels took him on an overland zigzag from Baghdad, through Iran to Bagram, Afghanistan. He has chronicled the experience in a series of vignettes, photographs and a short documentary film scheduled for independent release in 2013.

Benjamin Ditto travels the world with professional athletes in search of true adventure and unique imagery. Ditto is himself a talented climber and fits in well with the sports elite. The combination of being an athlete and a photographer allows him to go on very demanding expeditions to rarely visited areas and produce high quality images that capture the real action.

Cody Forest Doucette was born in the heartland of Wisconsin, raised in the mountains of Idaho and educated on the beaches of California at UCSB. He has spent the past 8 years chasing storms, light and laughter around the globe with his brother, writer Kitt Doucette. His work has appeared in numerous national and international publications including *Rolling Stone*, *Men's Journal*, *The Surfer's Journal*, *Powder* and *Dossier Journal*. For a complete portfolio please see his website at **codyforestdoucette.com**.

Paul Ferraris is a San Francisco based photographer and teacher. He loves snapping pictures of everything, and works best with natural light and film. He shoots with Mamiya 645 pro, Contax G2, Canon 5D MK2, and Canon 7D. His work has appeared in numerous books and publications such as *The Surfer's Journal*.

Ryan Libre is a 2010 Nikon Inspiration Award Winner, TED speaker, and grantee of the Pulitzer Center. Raised and educated in Northern California, he has called Asia home for over a decade. Ryan spends a lot of time getting to know his subjects and very little time post-processing. He went AWOL from the US Army and got a degree in Peace Studies. Ryan has held solo exhibitions throughout Japan. When not shooting or teaching photography, he enjoys working on his solar-powered homestead in northern Thailand.

Daniel Nahabedian is a former cubicle dweller who broke free from the corporate world to start a new career as a travel photographer. His work is focused on documenting different cultures to help break barriers and misunderstandings. Now settled in Chiang Mai, Thailand, he teaches photography, leads photowalks and works on his website "Canvas of Light" sharing photography tips with beginning photographers.

Aya Padrón loves going from place to place, scooping up muses and reveries as she moves. These she documents in drawings and pictures at **UnderTheSugar.com**.

Richard Stupart is a writer and photojournalist currently based in South Africa. His recent work has primarily focused on East African travel and stories of post-conflict recovery in Northern Uganda. In 2009, Richard journeyed solo from Cape Town to Cairo on public transport.

Paul Sullivan is a British journalist, author and photographer based in Berlin. His work has appeared in *The Guardian*, *The Independent*, *The Sunday Times* and *National Geographic UK*, and he is co-author / faculty member of the MatadorU photography program. He has been exploring the world independently for a decade.
Paul-Sullivan.com + PaulSullivan.PhotoShelter.com

EDITOR

David S. Miller is senior editor of Matador Network, winner of two Lowell Thomas awards for excellence in travel journalism.

BIBLIOGRAPHY

Adams, Douglas. *The Long Dark Tea-Time of the Soul.* New York: Simon & Schuster, 1991.

Apicella, Tim. *Flying Cows of Africa: Travel Stories from around the World.* Quoting Ray Bradbury. Bloomington, IN: iUniverse, 2009.

Angelou, Maya. *Wouldn't Taking Nothing for My Journey Now.* New York: Bantam, 1994.

Bade, William Frederic and Gifford, Terry. *John Muir: His Life and Letters and Other Writings.* Seattle: The Mountaineers, 1996.

Bashō Matsuo. *The Essential Basho.* Translated by Sam Hamill. Boston: Shambhala, 1999.

Battiste, Marie. *Reclaiming Indigenous Voice and Vision.* Quoting Chief Joseph. Vancouver: UBC Press, 2000.

Berry, Wendell. *The Unforeseen Wilderness: an essay on Kentucky's Red River Gorge.* Lexington, KY: University Press of Kentucky, 1971.

Borges, Jorge Luis. *The Aleph and Other Stories.* Translated by Andrew Hurley. New York: Penguin Classics, 2004.

Bryson, Bill. Editor's introduction to *The Best American Travel Writing 2000.* Boston: Houghton Mifflin, 2000.

Bukowski, Charles. *Erections, Ejaculations, Exhibitions, and General Tales of Ordinary Madness.* San Francisco: City Lights Books, 1972.

Buber, Martin. *The Legend of the Baal-Shem.* Princeton, NJ: Princeton University Press, 1995.

Byrd, Richard E. *Alone: The Classic Polar Adventure.* Washington, DC: Island Press, 2003.

Byrne, Robert. *1,911 best things anybody ever said.* Quoting Aldous Huxley. New York: Random House, 1988.

Cahill, Tim. *Road fever: a high-speed travelogue.* New York: Vintage Books, 1992.

Caldwell, Lee G. *The Fast Track to Profit.* Quoting Mario Andretti. Upper Saddle River, NJ: Prentice Hall Professional, 2003.

Calvino, Italo. *Invisible Cities.* Orlando, FL: Houghton Mifflin Harcourt, 1978.

Capote, Truman. *Other Voices, Other Rooms.* New York: Modern Library, 2004.

Cather, Willa. *O Pioneers!* Radford, Virginia: Wilder Publications, 2006.

Chekhov, Anton Pavlovich. *The Schoolmistress and other stories.* New York: Macmillan, 1921.

Chesterton, Gilbert Keith. *Tremendous Trifles.* New York: Dodd, Mead and Company, 1920.

Chouinard, Yvon. *Let My People Go Surfing: The Education of a Reluctant Businessman.* New York: Penguin, 2006.

Dickens, Charles. *Little Dorrit, Volume 1.* Leipzig: Bernhard Tauchnitz, 1856.

Disraeli, Benjamin. *Vivian Grey.* Philadelphia: E. L. Carey and A. Hart, 1837.

Duthel, Heinz. *Treasury of Wisdom Quotes.* Quoting Antoine de Saint Exupéry. Raleigh, NC: Lulu.com, 2008.

Elliott, Michael A. *Custerology.* Quoting "Curly." Chicago: University of Chicago Press, 2008.

Emerson, Ralph Waldo. *Selected Writings of Ralph Waldo Emerson.*
New York: New American Library, 2011.

Fanon, Frantz. *The wretched of the earth.* Preface by Jean-Paul Sartre. New York: Grove Press, 1968.

Fitzhenry, Robert I. *The Harper Book of Quotations.* Quoting Clifton Fadiman. New York: HarperCollins, 1993.

Fox, Matthew. *Creativity.* Quoting Pablo Neruda. New York: Penguin, 2004.

Friedlander, Shems. *The Whirling Dervishes.* Quoting Rumi. Albany: State University of New York, 1992.

Frost, Robert. *Robert Frost's Poems.* Edited by Louis Untermeyer.
New York: St. Martin's Paperbacks, 2002.

Green, Dudley. *Because It's There: The Life of George Mallory.* Gloucestershire, England: Tempus, 2005.

Gruwell, Erin and McCourt, Frank. *The Gigantic Book of Teachers' Wisdom.*
New York: Skyhorse Publishing, 2007.

Guthrie, Gary P. *1,600 Quotes and Pieces of Wisdom That Just Might Help You Out.* Quoting Mark Twain. Lincoln, NE: iUniverse, 2003.

Hamill, Sam. *The Poetry of Zen.* Translation of Li Po's "Zazen on Ching-t'ing Mountain."
Boston: Shambhala, 2004.

Harrison, Jim. *The Raw and the Cooked: Adventures of a Roving Gourmand.*
New York: Grove Press, 2001.

Haruo Shirane. *Early Modern Japanese Literature: An Anthology, 1600-1900.*
New York: Columbia University Press, 2002.

Hazlitt, William. *William Hazlitt, Essayist and Critic.* London: F. Warne, 1889.

Hotchner, A. E. *Papa Hemingway: A Personal Memoir.* Cambridge, MA: Da Capo Press, 2005.

Jarski, Rosemarie. *Words from the Wise: Over 6,000 of the Smartest Things Ever Said.* Quoting Carl Burns. New York: Skyhorse Publishing, 2007.

Jean de La Fontaine. *The Original Fables of La Fontaine.* Translated by F. C. Tilney.
Middlesex, England: Echo Library, 2006.

Jenkins, Mark. "The Ghost Road." In *The Best Travel Writing 2005*, edited by James O'Reilly, Sean O'Reilly, and Larry Habegger. Palo Alto, CA: Travelers' Tales, 2005.

Johnson, Samuel. *The Works of Samuel Johnson, L.L.D:Murphy's essay. The rambler.
The adventurer. The idler. Rasselas. Tales of the imagination. Letters. Irene. Miscellaneous poems.*
Charleston: Nabu Press, 2010.

Joyce, James. *A Portrait of the Artist as a Young Man.* New York: B. W. Huebsch, 1922.

Kazantzakis, Nikos. *Japan, China.* New York: Simon and Schuster, 1963.

Kerouac, Jack. *On the Road.* New York: Penguin, 2003.

Korzybski, Alfred. *Science and Sanity.* New York: Institute of General Semantics, 1994.

Kuchler, Bonnie Louise. *That's life: "wild" wit & wisdom*. Quoting Sir Edmund Hillary. Minocqua, WI: Willow Creek Press, 2003.

Kunitz, Stanley. "The Layers." *Passing Through: the later poems*. New York: W. W. Norton, 1997.

L'Amour, Louis. *Education of a Wandering Man*. New York: Random House Digital, 1989.

Lao Tzu. *Tao Te Ching: A New English Version, with Foreword and Notes by Stephen Mitchell*. New York: HarperCollins, 1991.

Levi, Primo. "Monday." In *Collected Poems*, translated by Ruth Feldman and Brian Swann. London: Faber and Faber, 1992.

Lewis, Sinclair. *Arrowsmith; Elmer Gantry; Dodsworth*. New York: Library of America, 2002.

London, Jack. *John Barleycorn*. New York: The Century, 1913.

Lopez, Barry. *About This Life: Journeys on the Threshold of Memory*. New York: Vintage Books, 1998.

MacKaye, Benton. "An Appalachian Trail: A Project in Regional Planning." In *Architectural Regionalism: Collected Writings on Place, Identity, Modernity, and Tradition*, edited by Vincent B. Canizaro. New York: Princeton Architectural Press, 2007.

Malandro, Loretta A. *Fearless Leadership: how to overcome behavioral blind spots and transform your organization*. Quoting Ralph Waldo Emerson. New York: McGraw-Hill Professional, 2009.

Martz, William J. *John Berryman*. Quoting the poem, "A Point of Age." St. Paul, MN: North Central Publishing, 1969.

Mead, Margaret. *Coming of Age in Samoa*. New York: HarperCollins, 2001.

Melville, Herman. *Moby Dick*. Edited by Mary R. Reichardt. San Francisco: Ignatius Press, 2011.

Messner, Reinhold. *All 14 Eight-Thousanders*. Seattle: The Mountaineers, 1999.

Miller, Henry. *Big Sur and the oranges of Hieronymus Bosch*. New York: New Directions, 1957.

Muir, John. *John Muir: the eight wilderness discovery books*. Seattle: The Mountaineers, 2004.

Moon, William Least Heat. *Blue Highways: A Journey into America*. New York: Fawcett Crest, 1984.

Peacock, Doug. *Grizzly Years: In Search of the American Wilderness*. New York: Holt Paperbacks, 1996.

Potts, Rolf. *Vagabonding: an uncommon guide to the art of long-term world travel*. Quoting Dagobert Runes. New York: Villard Books, 2002.

Proust, Marcel. *In Search of Lost Time*. Translated by C.K. Scott Moncrieff and Terence Kilmartin. Revised by D.J. Enright. New York: The Modern Library, 1992.

Rexroth, Kenneth. *One Hundred Poems from the Chinese*. Translation of Mei Yao Ch'en. New York: New Directions, 1971.

Rollyson, Carl Edmund and Paddock, Lisa Olson. *Susan Sontag: The Making of an Icon*. New York: W. W. Norton, 2000.

Roth, Eric H. and Aberson, Toni. *Compelling Conversations: Questions & Quotations on Timeless Topics*. Quoting G. K. Chesterton. Los Angeles: Chimayo Press, 2010.

Saint-Exupéry, Antoine de. *Wind, Sand and Stars*. Orlando, FL: Harcourt Brace, 1992.

Sangster, Rob and Leffel, Tim. *Traveler's Tool Kit: Mexico and Central America*. Quoting James Michener. Birmingham, AL: Minasha Ridge Press, 2008.

Shepard, Paul. *Man in the Landscape*. Athens, GA: University of Georgia Press, 2002.

Smith, Henry Percy and Johnson, Helen Kendrick. *A dictionary of terms, phrases, and quotations*. Quoting Carlo Goldoni. New York: D. Appleton and Company, 1895.

Snyder, Gary. *The Practice of the Wild: Essays*. San Francisco: North Point Press, 1990.

Stark, Freya. *Baghdad Sketches: Journeys Through Iraq*. London: Tauris Park Paperbacks, 2011.

Starrs, James E. *The Literary Cyclist: Great Bicycling Scenes in Literature*. Quoting Hemingway. New York: Breakaway Books, 1999.

Stecyk, Craig and Friedman, Glen E. *Dogtown: The Legend of the Z-Boys*. New York: Burning Flags Press, 2002.

Steinbeck, John. *Travels with Charley: in search of America*. New York: Penguin, 1997.

Stevenson, Robert Louis. *The Works of Robert Louis Stevenson: In the South Seas. Letters from Samoa, etc. Volume VII*. Edited by Charles Curtis Bigelow and Temple Scott. Boston: Young Folks' Educational League, 1908.

Stevenson, Robert Louis. *Travels with a Donkey in the Cévennes*. Boston: Roberts Brothers, 1879.

Steves, Rick. *Rick Steves' Europe Through the Back Door 2011*. Quoting Mohammed. Berkeley, CA: Avalon Travel, 2010.

Theroux, Paul. *The Tao of Travel: Enlightenments from Lives on the Road*. New York: Houghton Mifflin Harcourt, 2011.

Thompson, Hunter S. *Kingdom of Fear*. New York: Simon and Schuster, 2003.

Thompson, Will. *The Power of Play*. Quoting Plato. Bloomington, IN: AuthorHouse, 2006.

Thoreau, Henry David. *A Week on the Concord and Merrimack Rivers*. Boston: Ticknor and Fields, 1868.

Twain, Mark. *The Innocents Abroad*. New York: Penguin, 2002.

Twain, Mark. *Tom Sawyer abroad, Tom Sawyer, detective, and other stories*. New York: Harper & Brothers, 1923.

Vonnegut, Kurt. *Cat's Cradle*. New York: RosettaBooks, 2001.

Waits, Tom. *The Lyrics of Tom Waits: The Early Years*. New York: HarperCollins, 2007.

Warner, Charles Dudley. *Baddeck, and that sort of thing*. Boston: Houghton, Mifflin and Company, 1882.

Watts, Alan. *The Book: On the Taboo Against Knowing Who You Are*. New York: Random House Digital, 2011.

Whitehead, Alfred North. *Science and the Modern World*. New York: Simon and Schuster, 1997.

Whitman, Walt. "Song of the Open Road." In *Critical Companion to Walt Whitman*, by Charles M. Oliver. New York: Infobase Publishing, 2006.

Wilde, Oscar. *The Importance of Being Earnest and Other Plays*. New York: Simon and Schuster, 2005.

Williamson, Karen. *Sleep Deep: Simple Techniques for Beating Insomnia*. Quoting Einstein. New York: Penguin, 2007.

"Every day is a journey,
and the journey itself is home."
– MATSUO BASHŌ